GOSPEL • HYMNS •

58 Songs 1

EVERLASTING
PRAISE

A Timeless Resource
for Congregation and Choir

Compiled and Arranged by

MIKE SPECK &
RUSSELL MAULDIN

LILLENAS
PUBLISHING COMPANY

TRUSTING GOD

includes
I Will Say of the Lord
Leaning on the Everlasting Arms
'Tis So Sweet to Trust in Jesus

*Arranged by Mike Spec
and Russell Mauldi*

Presentation Suggestions:
I WILL SAY OF THE LORD: Parts, repeat ending, medley ending
LEANING ON THE EVERLASTING ARMS: Unison, medley ending
'TIS SO SWEET TO TRUST IN JESUS: Parts; Ms.70, unison, medley ending; Ms.81,
parts, 1st and 2nd endings

I Will Say of the Lord

Words and Music b
JOHN SYLVESTER FEARI
*Arranged by Mike Spec
and Russell Mauldi*

Leaning on the Everlasting Arms

LISHA A. HOFFMAN

ANTHONY J. SHOWALTER
*Arranged by Mike Speck
and Russell Mauldin*

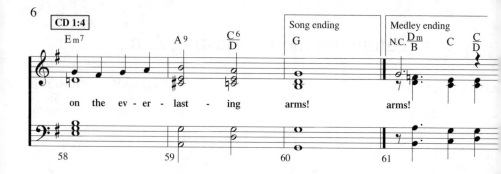

'Tis So Sweet to Trust in Jesus

LOUISA M. R. STEAD

WILLIAM J. KIRKPATRICK
Arranged by Mike Speck
and Russell Mauldin

JESUS LIVES

includes
He Lives
Jesus Is Alive and Well
Jesus Is Alive
Because He Lives

Arranged by Mike Spec
and Russell Mauldi

Presentation Suggestions:
HE LIVES: Parts; Ms. 6, beat 4, unison; Ms. 12, parts; Ms. 15, beat 4, unison (optional ocatves); Ms. 19, parts, medley ending; Ms. 22, beat 4, unison
JESUS IS ALIVE AND WELL: Unison; Ms. 30, beat 4, parts; Ms. 41, unison, medley ending; Ms. 49, beat 4, parts; Ms. 60, unison, medley ending
JESUS IS ALIVE: Parts; Ms. 69, unison; Ms. 76, beat 3, parts; Pickup to Ms. 83, unison; Ms. 90, beat 3, parts, medley ending
BECAUSE HE LIVES: Unison; Ms. 111, parts, medley ending; Ms. 120, unison; Ms. 124, parts

He Lives

Words and Music b
ALFRED H. ACKLE
Arranged by Mike Spec
and Russell Mauldi

Medley Sequence copyright © 2004 by PsalmSinger Music (BMI) and Pilot Point Music (ASCAP). All rights reserved.
Administered by The Copyright Company, 1025 16th Avenue South, Nashville, TN 37212.

PLEASE NOTE: Copying of this product is NOT covered by CCLI licenses. For CCLI information call 1-800-234-2446.

12

Jesus Is Alive and Well

Words and Music b
BETTE JEAN ROBINSO
Arranged by Mike Spe
and Russell Mauld

13

14

Jesus Is Alive

Words and Music by
RON KENOLY
*Arranged by Mike Speck
and Russell Mauldin*

Hal - le - lu - jah!

Je - sus is a - live, Death has lost its vic -

- t'ry and the grave has been de - nied;

Je - sus lives for - ev - er, He's a - live,

CD 1:11

Because He Lives

GLORIA GAITHER and
WILLIAM J. GAITHER

WILLIAM J. GAITHER
*Arranged by Mike Speck
and Russell Mauldin*

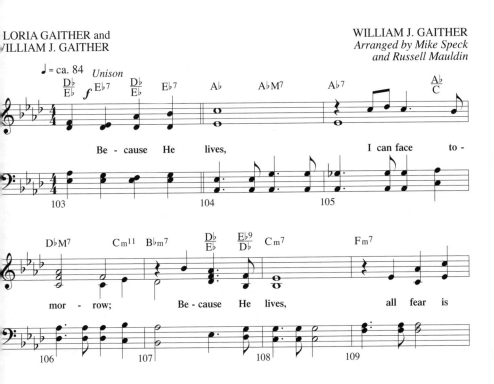

18

COME TO WORSHIP

includes
Come, Now Is the Time to Worship
Here I Am to Worship
We Have Come to Worship Jesus

*Arranged by Mike Speck
and Russell Mauldin*

Presentation Suggestions:
   COME, NOW IS THE TIME TO WORSHIP: Unison; Ms. 23, parts, 1st & 2nd
      endings; D.S., Ms. 5, unison; Coda, medley ending
   HERE I AM TO WORSHIP: Parts, repeat ending, medley ending
   WE HAVE COME TO WORSHIP JESUS: Unison; Ms. 58, parts, repeat ending; Ms.
      65, unison; Ms. 58, parts, medley ending

Come, Now Is the Time to Worship

Words and Music by
BRIAN DOERKSEN
*Arranged by Mike Speck
and Russell Mauldin*

One day ev - 'ry knee____ will bow.____

Still the great - est trea - sure re - mains____ for those____ Who glad -

CD 1:16 1st time

- ly choose____ You now.____

CD 1:17

D.S. al Coda ⊕ CODA

come.

Come. rit.

Song ending
Come.

Medley ending
Come.

Here I Am to Worship

Words and Music
TIM HUGHES
Arranged by Mike Speck
and Russell Maule

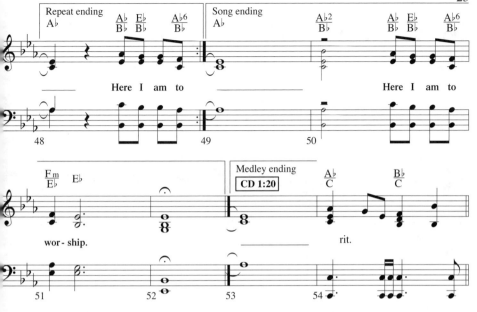

We Have Come to Worship Jesus

Words and Music by
MARK CHADWICK
*Arranged by Mike Speck
and Russell Mauldin*

HEAVENBOUND

includes

Since Jesus Came into My Heart
He Set Me Free
When We All Get to Heaven
What a Day That Will Be

Arranged by Mike Speck
and Russell Mauldin

Presentation Suggestions:
 SINCE JESUS CAME INTO MY HEART: Verse 1, unison; Ms. 11, beat 3, parts,
 medley ending
 HE SET ME FREE: Parts, repeat ending, medley ending
 WHEN WE ALL GET TO HEAVEN: Verse 1, unison; Ms. 44, beat 4, parts, medley
 ending; Ms. 63, beat 4, unison; Ms. 65, beat 2, parts
 WHAT A DAY THAT WILL BE: Parts, medley ending

Since Jesus Came into My Heart

RUFUS H. MCDANIEL

CHARLES H. GABRIEL
Arranged by Mike Speck
and Russell Mauldin

1. What a won - der - ful change in my life has been wrought Since
2. I have ceased from my wan - d'ring and go - ing a - stray Since
3. I'm pos - sessed of a hope that is stead - fast and sure, Since
4. There's a light in the val - ley of death now for me, Since
5. I shall go there to dwell in that cit - y I know, Since

CD 1:23

Je - sus came in - to my heart! I have
Je - sus came in - to my heart; And my
Je - sus came in - to my heart; And no
Je - sus came in - to my heart; And the
Je - sus came in - to my heart; And I'm

light in my soul for which long I had sought, Since
sins which were man - y are all washed a - way, Since
dark clouds of doubt now my path - way ob - scure, Since
gates of the cit - y be - yond I can see, Since
hap - py, so hap - py, as on - ward I go, Since

Parts

Je - sus came in - to my heart!
Je - sus came in - to my heart.
Je - sus came in - to my heart.
Je - sus came in - to my heart.
Je - sus came in - to my heart.

Since

Je - sus came in - to my heart, Since

CD 1:24 2nd time

Repeat ending | Song ending | Medley ending

He Set Me Free

Words and Music by
ALBERT E. BRUMLEY
*Arranged by Mike Speck
and Russell Mauldin*

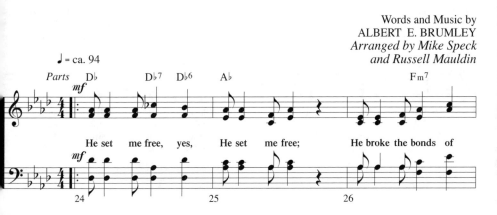

When We All Get to Heaven

ELIZA E. HEWITT

EMILY D. WILSON
Arranged by Mike Speck
and Russell Mauldin

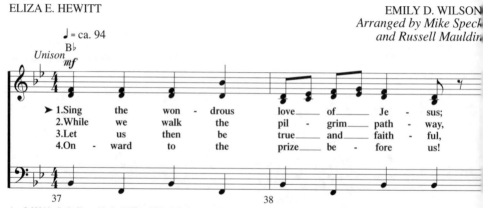

1. Sing the won - drous love of Je - sus;
2. While we walk the pil - grim path - way,
3. Let us then be true and faith - ful,
4. On - ward to the prize be - fore us!

30

What a Day That Will Be

Words and Music by
JIM HILL
*Arranged by Mike Speck
and Russell Mauldin*

RISE UP AND PRAISE

includes
Rise Up and Praise Him
Praise the Name of Jesus
Shout to the Lord

Arranged by Mike Speck
and Russell Mauldin

Presentation Suggestions:
RISE UP AND PRAISE HIM: Unison; Pickup to Ms. 23, parts; Ms. 32, beat 2, unison;
Pickup to Ms. 35, parts, repeat; Ms. 32, beat 2, unison; Pickup to Ms. 35, parts; Ms.
36, unison,medley ending
PRAISE THE NAME OF JESUS:Parts; Ms.56, unison, medley ending
SHOUT TO THE LORD: Ladies unison; Ms. 72, choir unison; Ms. 80, parts; Ms. 85,
beat 4, unison, medley ending; Ms. 96, parts

Rise Up and Praise Him

Words and Music by
PAUL BALOCHE
and GARY SADLER
Arranged by Mike Speck
and Russell Mauldin

35

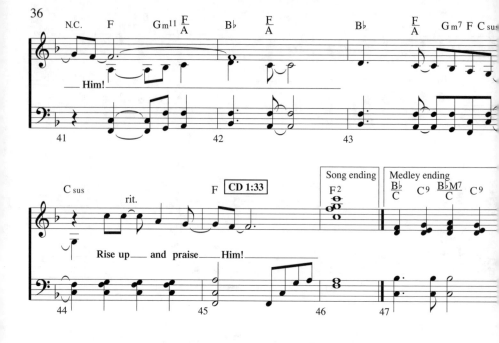

Praise the Name of Jesus

Words and Music by
ROY HICKS, JR.
Arranged by Mike Spec
and Russell Mauldi

He's my De-liv-er-er; in Him will I trust. Praise the name of

Je - sus. Je - sus.

Praise the name of Je - sus.

Shout to the Lord

Words and Music by
DARLENE ZSCHECH
*Arranged by Mike Speck
and Russell Mauldin*

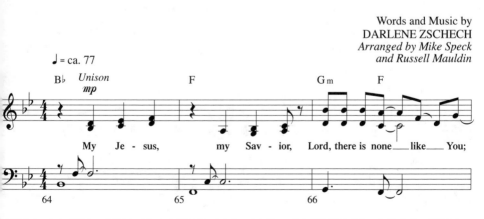

My Je - sus, my Sav - ior, Lord, there is none___ like___ You;

40

THE CROSS OF CALVARY

includes
I Will Sing of My Redeemer
At Calvary
It Is Well with My Soul
The Wonderful Cross *with* He Looked Beyond My Fault

Arranged by Mike Speck
and Russell Mauldin

Presentation Suggestions:
I WILL SING OF MY REDEEMER: Verse 1, unison; Ms. 13, parts, repeat ending,
  medley ending
AT CALVARY: Unison, medley ending
IT IS WELL WITH MY SOUL: Verse 3, solo; Ms. 54, beat 3, solo w/choir parts;
  Ms.58, beat 3, parts, medley ending
THE WONDERFUL CROSS: Parts; Ms. 67, beat 3, unison; Ms. 71, beat 3, parts; Ms.
  75, beat 3, unison; Ms. 91, parts; Ms. 95, beat 3, unison; Ms. 99, beat 3, parts

I Will Sing of My Redeemer

HILIP P. BLISS

JAMES MCGRANAHAN
Arranged by Mike Speck
and Russell Mauldin

$\quad$ = ca. 98

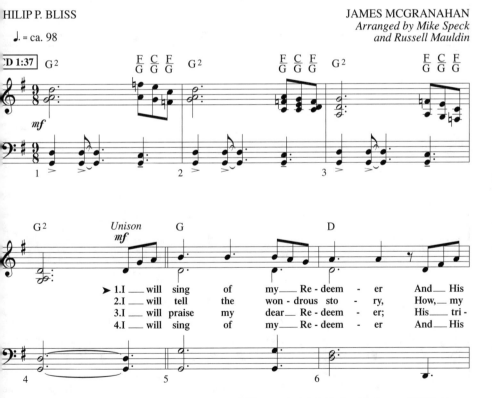

44

At Calvary

WILLIAM R. NEWELL

DANIEL B. TOWNE
Arranged by Mike Spe
and Russell Maula

It Is Well with My Soul

RATIO G. SPAFFORD

PHILIP P. BLISS
Arranged by Mike Speck
and Russell Mauldin

The Wonderful Cross
with
He Looked Beyond My Fault

ISAAC WATTS, CHRIS TOMLIN,
JESSE REEVES and J. D. WALT

LOWELL MASON, CHRIS TOMLIN,
JESSE REEVES and J. D. WALT
*Arranged by Mike Speck
and Russell Mauldin*

48

OUR GOD IS MIGHTY

includes
Mighty Is Our God
Blessed Be the Lord God Almighty
To Him Who Sits on the Throne
Who Can Satisfy My Soul

Arranged by Mike Spe[c]
and Russell Mauld[i]

Presentation Suggestions:
MIGHTY IS OUR GOD: Parts; Ms. 21, beat 2, unison; Ms. 27, beat 3 1/2, parts; D.S.,
  coda-medley ending; Ms. 36, unison
BLESSED BE THE LORD GOD ALMIGHTY: Unison/parts as indicated, medley
  ending, medley ending
TO HIM WHO SITS ON THE THRONE: Unison; Ms. 70, beat 3, parts; Ms. 78, beat 3,
  unison; Ms. 81, parts; Ms. 82, beat 3, unison; medley ending, parts
WHO CAN SATISFY MY SOUL: Parts, medley ending, medley ending

Mighty Is Our God

Words and Music b[y]
EUGENE GREC[O]
GERRIT GUSTAFSON and DON MOE[N]
Arranged by Mike Spe[c]
and Russell Mauld[i]

52

Blessed Be the Lord God Almighty

Words and Music by
BOB FITTS
*Arranged by Mike Speck
and Russell Mauldin*

To Him Who Sits on the Throne

Words and Music by
DEBBYE GRAAFSMA
Arranged by Mike Speck
and Russell Mauldin

56

Who Can Satisfy My Soul

Words and Music by
DENNIS JERNIGAN
Arranged by Mike Speck
and Russell Mauldin

WORSHIP HIS MAJESTY

includes
Majesty
How Great Thou Art

*Arranged by Mike Speck
and Russell Mauldin*

Presentation Suggestions:
  MAJESTY: Parts/unison as indicated, medley ending
  HOW GREAT THOU ART: Parts; Ms. 47, unison; Ms. 51, parts, medley ending

Majesty

Words and Music by
JACK HAYFORD
*Arranged by Mike Speck
and Russell Mauldin*

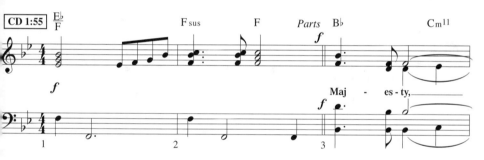

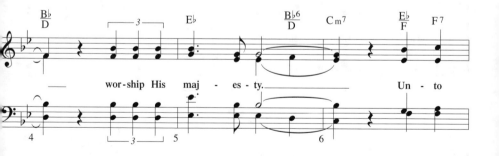

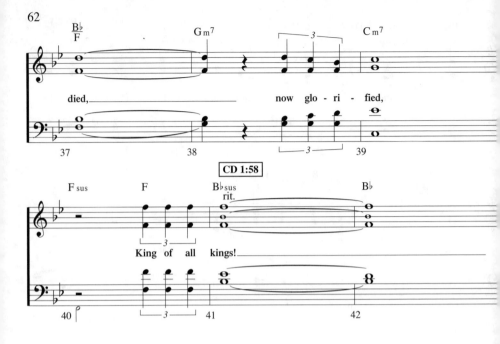

How Great Thou Art

Words and Music b
STUART K. HINE
*Arranged by Mike Spec
and Russell Mauldi*

WE WILL TESTIFY

includes
Testify
Let the Redeemed

Arranged by Mike Spe...
and Russell Mauld...

Presentation Suggestions:
TESTIFY: Parts; Ms. 16, unison, repeat ending; Ms. 24, parts; Ms. 16, unison, medley ending
LET THE REDEEMED: Parts, repeat ending, medley ending; Ms. 57, unison, 1st ending; Ms. 65, parts; Ms. 57, unison, 2nd ending; Ms. 74, parts
TESTIFY - Optional Reprise: begin at Ms. 48, parts/unison as before.

Testify

Words and Music t...
DOTTIE PEOPLE...
Arranged by Mike Spe...
and Russell Mauld...

Medley Sequence copyright © 2004 by PsalmSinger Music (BMI) and Pilot Point Music (ASCAP). All rights reserved.
Administered by The Copyright Company, 1025 16th Avenue South, Nashville, TN 37212.

PLEASE NOTE: Copying of this product is NOT covered by CCLI licenses. For CCLI information call 1-800-234-2446.

Let the Redeemed

Words and Music b
WARD ELLI
Arranged by Mike Spe
and Russell Mauld

HE'S WORTHY

includes
He's Worthy
Great Is the Lord
Ancient of Days

*Arranged by Mike Speck
and Russell Mauldin*

Presentation Suggestions:
HE'S WORTHY: Parts, 1st ending, 2nd ending, repeat ending, medley ending
GREAT IS THE LORD: Unison; Ms. 33, parts, medley ending; Ms. 52, beat 2, unison
ANCIENT OF DAYS: Parts; Ms. 72, beat 2, unison, 1st ending; Ms. 65, parts; Ms. 72,
   beat 2, unison, 2nd ending

He's Worthy

Words and Music by
SANDRA CROUCH
*Arranged by Mike Speck
and Russell Mauldin*

Great Is the Lord

Words and Music by
MICHAEL W. SMITH
and DEBORAH D. SMITH
*Arranged by Mike Speck
and Russell Mauldin*

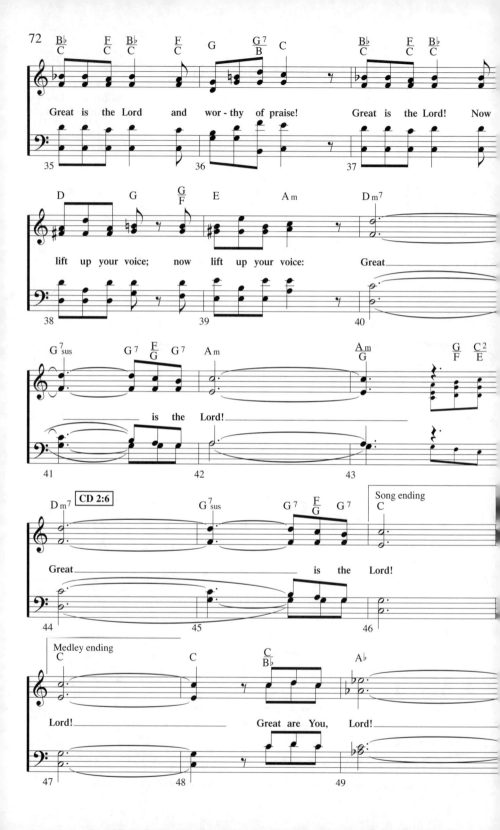

Ancient of Days

Words and Music by
JAMIE HARVILL and GARY SADLER
Arranged by Mike Speck
and Russell Mauldin

You will be ex - alt - ed, O God, and Your

king - dom shall not pass a - way, O An - cient of Days.

O An-cient of Days.

O An - cient of Days!

CD 2:9 1st time

POWER IN THE BLOOD

includes

There Is Power in the Blood
The Blood Will Never Lose Its Power
What the Lord Has Done in Me

Arranged by Mike Spec
and Russell Mauld

Presentation Suggestions:
THERE IS POWER IN THE BLOOD: Verse 1, unison/parts as indicated, repeat
ending; Verse 2, unison/parts as indicated, medley ending
THE BLOOD WILL NEVER LOSE ITS POWER: Unison; Ms. 39, parts; Ms. 49,
Solo; Pickup to Ms. 66, choir parts, medley ending
WHAT THE LORD HAS DONE IN ME: Verse 1, unison; Ms. 100, beat 3, parts; Ms.
106, beat 3, 2-part choir as indicated, 1st ending; Ms. 108, beat 3, parts; Ms. 106,
beat 3, 2-part choir, medley ending; Ms. 113, ladies unison; Ms. 122, choir unison;
Ms. 126, beat 3, 2-part choir; Ms. 129, parts; Ms. 137, beat 3, 2-part choir, 1st
ending; Ms. 139, beat 3, parts; Ms. 137, beat 3, 2-part choir, 2nd ending; Ms. 143,
beat 3, parts

There Is Power in the Blood

Words and Music b
LEWIS E. JONE
Arranged by Mike Spec
and Russell Mauld

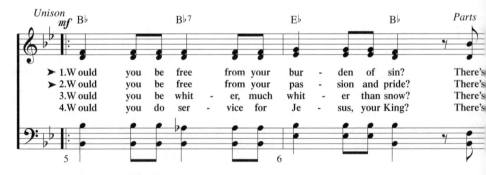

pow'r, pow'r, won-der-work-ing pow'r In the blood_____ of the

Lamb. There is pow'r, pow'r, won-der-work-ing pow'r In the

pre - cious blood of the Lamb._____

The Blood Will Never Lose Its Power

Words and Music by
ANDRAE CROUCH
Arranged by Mike Spec
and Russell Mauldin

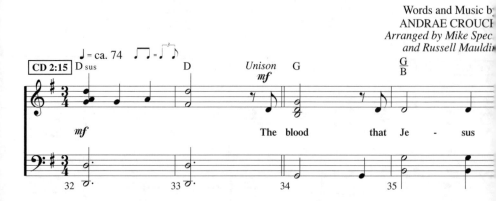

The blood that Je - sus

80

What the Lord Has Done in Me

Words and Music by
REUBEN MORGAN
*Arranged by Mike Speck
and Russell Mauldin*

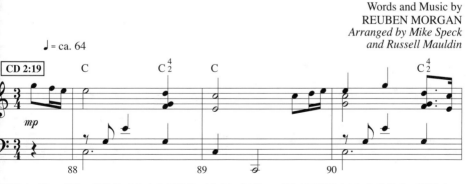

JESUS THE KING

includes
All Hail the Power of Jesus' Name
Victory Chant
The King of Who I Am
O for a Thousand Tongues

Arranged by Mike Speck
and Russell Mauldin

Presentation Suggestions:
ALL HAIL THE POWER OF JESUS' NAME: Verse 1, unison; Ms. 9, beat 4, parts;
  Ms. 13, beat 4, unison; Ms. 16, parts; Ms. 17, unison, medley ending
VICTORY CHANT: Verse 1, leader/group as indicated, medley ending; Ms. 30,
  leader/group as indicated
THE KING OF WHO I AM: Unison, Ms. 62, parts; Ms. 64, unison; pickup to Ms. 65,
  parts; pickup to Ms. 67, unison, medley ending; pickup to Ms. 70, parts
O FOR A THOUSAND TONGUES: Parts; Ms. 83, unison, medley ending; Ms. 95,
  beat 3, parts; Ms. 99, unison; Ms. 101, parts

All Hail the Power of Jesus' Name

)WARD PERRONET

OLIVER HOLDEN
Arranged by Mike Speck
and Russell Mauldin

♩= ca. 98

86

Victory Chant

Words and Music by
JOSEPH VOGELS
*Arranged by Mike Speck
and Russell Mauldin*

1.Hail, Je - sus, You're my King.
2.Hail, Je - sus, You're my Lord.
3.Glo - ry, glo - ry to the Lamb.

Hail, Je - sus, You're my King. Your life_ frees me to sing.
Hail, Je - sus, You're my Lord. I will_ o - bey Your Word.
Glo - ry, glo - ry to the Lamb. You take me in - to the Land.

Your life_ frees me to sing._ I will praise_ You all my days._
I will_ o - bey Your Word. I want to see_ Your King - dom come. I
You take me in - to the Land._ We will con - quer in Your name._

I will praise_ You all my days. Per - fect_ in all Your ways.
want to see_ Your King - dom come. Not my will, but Yours be done.
We will con - quer in Your name. And pro - claim that Je - sus reigns.

The King of Who I Am

Words and Music by
TANYA GOODMAN
and MICHAEL SYKES
*Arranged by Mike Speck
and Russell Mauldin*

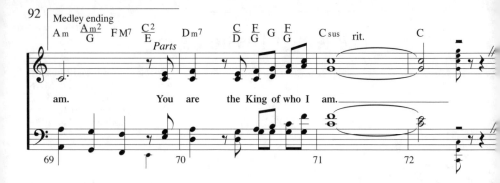

O for a Thousand Tongues

Words and Music by
DAVID BINION
*Arranged by Mike Speck
and Russell Mauldin*

COME INTO THE HOUSE

includes
House of the Lord
We Have Come into His House
O Come, Let Us Adore Him

Arranged by Mike Spec
and Russell Mauldi

Presentation Suggestions:
  HOUSE OF THE LORD: Parts, repeat ending, medley ending
  WE HAVE COME INTO HIS HOUSE: Verse 1, unison, medley ending; Ms. 33, parts,
  1st ending, 2nd ending; Ms. 45, unison
  O COME, LET US ADORE HIM: Verse 1, unison, medley ending; Ms. 60, parts

House of the Lord

Words and Music b
JOHN DARIN ROWSE
Arranged by Mike Spec
and Russell Mauldi

95

Gath-ered in one ac-cord,

Let the peo-ple re-joice in the house of the Lord.

CD 2:34 / 2:35 1st / 2nd time

Repeat ending
Eb

Song ending
Eb

Medley ending
Eb

We Have Come into His House

Words and Music by
BRUCE BALLINGER
*Arranged by Mike Speck
and Russell Mauldin*

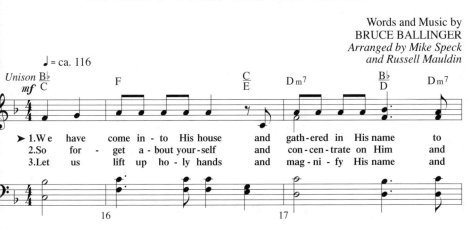

♩ = ca. 116

Unison
mf

➤ 1. We have come in-to His house and gath-ered in His name to
2. So for-get a-bout your-self and con-cen-trate on Him and
3. Let us lift up ho-ly hands and mag-ni-fy His name and

Wel- come to the house of the Lord,_____ It's a house filled with praise,

a house filled with joy._____

Gath - ered in one____ ac - cord,_____ Let the peo - ple re - joice____

_____ in the house of the Lord._____

Gath - ered in one____ ac - cord,_____ Let the peo - ple re - joice____

98

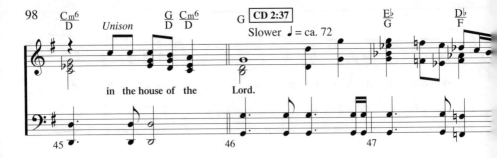

O Come, Let Us Adore Him

JOHN F. WADE
and others

JOHN F. WAD[E]
Arranged by Mike Spe[e]
and Russell Maula[ldin]

GOD'S LOVE

includes
My Savior's Love
The Love of God
You Are My King
At the Cross

Arranged by Mike Spe
and Russell Maula

Presentation Suggestions:
 MY SAVIOR'S LOVE: Verse 1, unison; Ms. 13, parts, repeat ending, medley ending
 THE LOVE OF GOD: Verse 3, solo; Ms. 44, beat 2, choir parts, medley ending
 YOU ARE MY KING: Unison; Ms. 66, parts, repeat ending, medley ending
 AT THE CROSS: Unison, medley ending. Ms. 90, parts

My Savior's Love

Words and Music
CHARLES H. GABRIE
Arranged by Mike Spe
and Russell Maula

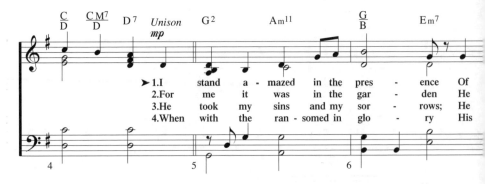

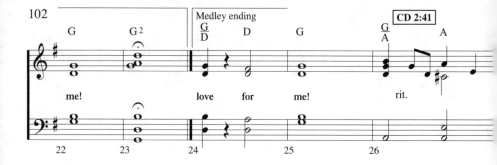

The Love of God

FREDERICK M. LEHMAN and
MEIR BEN ISAAC NEHORAI

FREDERICK M. LEHMA
Arranged by Mike Spe
and Russell Mauld

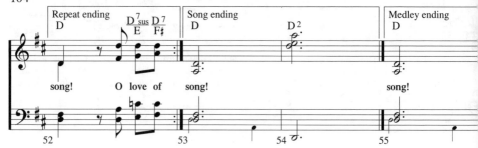

You Are My King

Words and Music by
BILLY JAMES FOOTE
Arranged by Mike Speck
and Russell Mauldin

It's my joy___ to hon - or You.___ In all___ I

do, I hon-or You. In all___ I do, I hon-or

Repeat ending You. Song ending You. Medley ending You.

At the Cross

ISAAC WATTS

RALPH E. HUDSON
Arranged by Mike Spe...
and Russell Mauld...

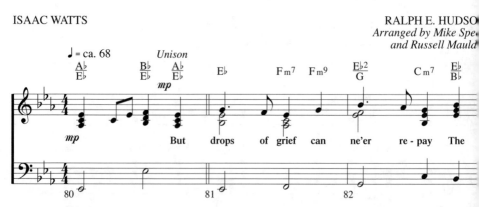

But drops of grief can ne'er re - pay The

108

GOD IS HOLY

includes
Because We Believe
Holy, Holy, Holy! Lord God Almighty

Arranged by Mike Speck
and Russell Mauldin

Presentation Suggestions:
    BECAUSE WE BELIEVE: Verse 1, leader/group unison as indicated, 1st ending;
    Verse 2, leader/group unison, 2nd ending; Ms. 14, parts; Pickup to Ms. 25, unison,
    medley ending; Ms. 31, leader/group unison; Ms. 39, parts; Pickup to Ms. 50,
    unison, repeat ending; Ms. 39, parts; Pickup to Ms. 50, unison, medley ending
    HOLY, HOLY, HOLY! LORD GOD ALMIGHTY: Verse 4, unison/parts as indicated,
    medley ending; Ms. 76, parts

Because We Believe

Words and Music by
JAMIE HARVILL and
NANCY GORDON
Arranged by Mike Speck
and Russell Mauldin

CD 2:48 ♩ = ca. 81

1.We be-lieve___ in___ God the Fa - ther, We be-lieve___ in___ God, the Fa - ther,
2.We be-lieve___ in the Ho - ly Bib - le, We be-lieve___ in the Ho - ly Bib - le,
3.We be-lieve___ in the blood of Je - sus, We be-lieve___ in the blood of Je - sus,

Leader

Db2   Cb2   Db2   **Group**   Cb2   Db2

We be-lieve___ in e - ter - nal life,   We be-lieve___ in e - ter - nal life,

33   34

Leader

GbM9   **Group**

We be-lieve___ in His blood that frees___ us,   We be-lieve___ in His blood that frees___ us,

35   36

CD 2:52

Leader

Db2   Cb2   Db2   **Group**   Cb2   Db2

To be-come___ the___ bride of Christ.   To be-come___ the___ bride of Christ.

37   38

Gb2   *Parts*   Ab/Db   Gb2   Ab   Db

f

Ho - ly,   ho - ly,   ho - ly   is   our God;

f

39   40

Db   Eb/Db   Db   Dbsus/Eb   Db2/F   Gb2   Ab/Db

Wor-thy, wor - thy,

41   42   43

Holy, Holy, Holy! Lord God Almighty

REGINALD HEBER

JOHN B. DYKE
Arranged by Mike Spe
and Russell Mauld

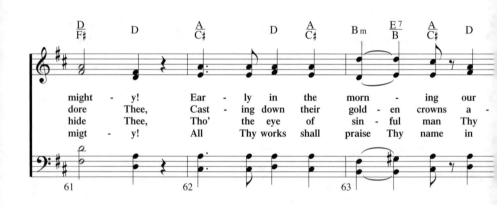

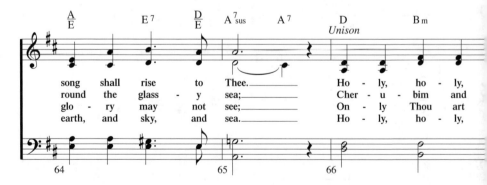

OUR ALL IN ALL

includes

My Life Is in You, Lord
You Are My All in All
I Worship You, Almighty God

Arranged by Mike Spe
and Russell Maula

Presentation Suggestions:
MY LIFE IS IN YOU, LORD: Parts; Ms. 24, beat 4, unison; Ms. 40, beat 4, parts, D.S.
to Ms. 9, coda, medley ending
YOU ARE MY ALL IN ALL: Verse 1, men unison; Ms. 51, ladies unison; Ms. 55,
choir parts, repeat ending; Verse 2, men unison; Ms. 51, ladies unison; Ms. 55, choir
parts, medley ending; Ms. 65, unison
I WORSHIP YOU, ALMIGHTY GOD: Parts/unison as indicated, medley ending

My Life Is in You, Lord

Words and Music
DANIEL GARDNE
Arranged by Mike Spe
and Russell Maula

118

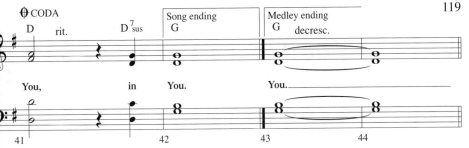

You Are My All in All

Words and Music by
DENNIS JERNIGAN
*Arranged by Mike Speck
and Russell Mauldin*

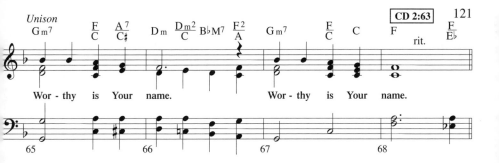

I Worship You, Almighty God

Words and Music by
SONDRA CORBETT
*Arranged by Mike Speck
and Russell Mauldin*

122 *Parts*

124

GOD DOES GREAT THINGS

includes
To God Be the Glory
Thank You, Lord
When I Think About the Lord

Arranged by Mike Spec
and Russell Mauldi

Presentation Suggestions:
TO GOD BE THE GLORY: Parts; Ms. 12, beat 3, unison; Ms. 16, beat 3, parts,
medley ending; Ms. 30, beat 3, unison; Ms. 34, beat 3, parts, medley ending
THANK YOU, LORD: Unison; Ms. 50, beat 5, parts, Repeat ending, medley ending;
Ms. 72, beat 4, unison
WHEN I THINK ABOUT THE LORD: Unison/parts as indicated, with repeats

To God Be the Glory

FANNY J. CROSBY

WILLIAM H. DOAN
Arranged by Mike Spec
and Russell Mauldi

125

Thank You, Lord

Words and Music by
DENNIS JERNIGAN
Arranged by Mike Spec
and Russell Mauldi

128

CD 2:70

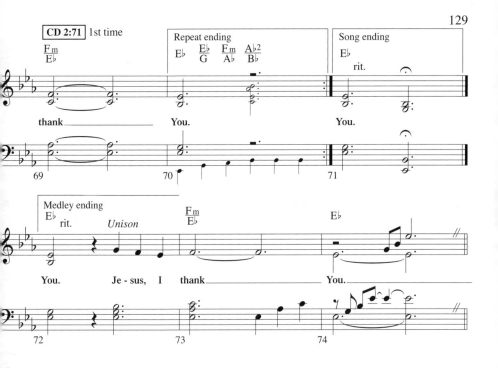

When I Think About the Lord

Words and Music by
JAMES HUEY
*Arranged by Mike Speck
and Russell Mauldin*

filled me___ with the Ho - ly Ghost,___ how He healed me___ to th

ut - ter-most;___ When I think a - bout___ the Lord,_____ how H

picked me up___ and turned___ me a - round,___ how He placed my feet___

CD 2:76

___ on sol - id ground._____ It makes me wan - na sho

Parts

___ Ha - le - lu - jah, thank You Je

THE LAST DAYS

includes
Soon and Very Soon
Days of Elijah
The King Is Coming

Arranged by Mike Speck
and Russell Mauldin

Presentation Suggestions:
SOON AND VERY SOON: Verse 1, parts; Ms. 16, beat 4, unison; Ms. 18, beat 4,
  parts, 1st ending; verse 1, parts; Ms. 16, beat 4, unison; Ms. 18, beat 4, parts; 2nd
  ending, unison/parts as indicated, medley ending
DAYS OF ELIJAH: Verse 1, unison; Ms. 49, beat 2, parts, repeat ending; verse 2,
  unison; Ms. 49, beat 2, parts, medley ending, medley ending
THE KING IS COMING: Parts, medley ending; Ms. 92, beat 3, unison; Ms. 95 parts

Soon and Very Soon

Words and Music by
ANDRAE CROUCH
Arranged by Mike Speck
and Russell Mauldin

Days of Elijah

Words and Music by
ROBIN MARK
*Arranged by Mike Speck
and Russell Mauldin*

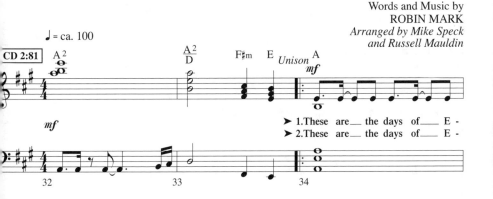

> 1.These are the days of E -
> 2.These are the days of E -

140

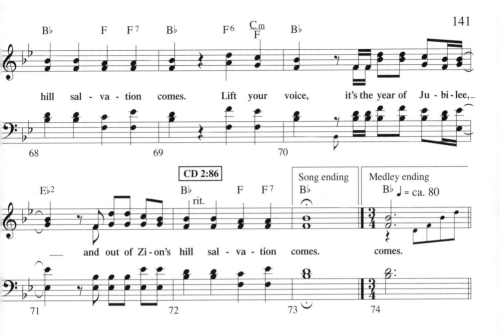

hill sal - va - tion comes. Lift your voice, it's the year of Ju - bi - lee,

_____ and out of Zi - on's hill sal - va - tion comes. comes.

The King Is Coming

GLORIA GAITHER, WILLIAM J. GAITHER
and CHARLES MILHUFF

WILLIAM J. GAITHER
Arranged by Mike Speck
and Russell Mauldin

The King_____ is com - ing! The King_____ is com - ing! I just heard the trum - pet

142

FOR INFORMATION AND BOOKINGS CONTACT:
Mike Speck Ministries
P. O. Box 2609
Lebanon, TN 37088
(615) 449-1888

Alphabetical Index
Song and MEDLEY Titles